Echoes Of My Mind

Vera Ann Yap

I don't know who I'm supposed to be

I don't know what I want to be, who I want to be

I'm lost, my mind overthinks

I can't stop the thoughts from overflowing my head

All I can do is stare

I watched blankly at the drywall, it was so white

I began to zone out, as the world went by

But I'm unable to move, unable to utter a sound

So, I let the thoughts just fill my mind

To the point that it starts to overflow

Like a statue, I can't seem to move

My mind seems to be in another universe

I snap out of it; I don't know what just happened

I don't know how I feel, but now I'd resumed back to my life

No longer zoned out, staring at the drywall

It's late, the sky is pitch black

There are no stars because the world is polluted

I'm reminded of you, we used to stay up late

Just chatting, but we don't do that anymore

I still do that, but now, I read and write

I can't sleep, it tough, I can't seem to turn my mind off

I tend to overthink, mostly when I'm alone

I can't sleep until I can

She was a hopeless romantic

Always watch romance movies

Reading romantic books, writing stories that had happy
endings

She was a hopeless romantic

She was a hopeless romantic

But not anymore

Her whole life she thought about the life she wanted

The kind of romance on screens

She had to stop being a hopeless romantic

To see the world as it was

But she still reads and writes about them

Living in her world, where she could escape life

She was not a hopeless romantic, she had stopped playing
fantasy

I'm the girl who can't seem to make friends

I'm the girl that fell for a silly boy

A girl who had her heart broken by the same boy she fell for

I'm a girl that's lonely and sad inside

I'm the girl that had her heart broken by one too many boys

The girl who broke a boy's heart, because she started pushing people away

The girl who after all this time, still can't seem to make any friends

I'm dealing with this void inside of me, that seems to never end

The girl who can't trust, the girl with too many problems to count

I'm the girl that cares too damn much, the girl that not many guys want

I'm the girl that is too damn shy to make any new friends

The sad, lonely, in her-world kind of girl

She's the kind of woman who stays, despite the pain

Her heart is a canvas of bruises, yet she remains

Loyal and steadfast, through every storm

Her love, a flame that flickers, but never loses its light

With a heart that's been hurt, she still loves with all her might

A hopeful romantic, she longs for that without a doubt

A love that endures, through laughter and tears

A bond that strengthens, through all the passing years

She wants to love without bounds, with every fibre of her soul

A love that shines bright, and never loses its goal

But she has been hurt one too many times

Still, her heart remains pure, one-of-a-kind

You pour your heart and soul into others, filling their cups to the brim

A kind and gentle spirit, with a love that's pure and slim

But not everyone shares your heart of gold

Some hearts are different, with love that's grown cold

You love with every fibre of your being, holding nothing back

While others offer only half their hearts, with a blank love

You give them the sweetest ingredients, expecting a delicious treat

But in return, you get a bitter taste, a smoothie that's undrinkable and beat

Not everyone is like you, with a heart that's true and kind

Not everyone knows how to blend love that's one-of-a-kind

You deserve an equal love, a divine smoothie

One that will quench your thirst, and forever be on your mind

You're her best friend, I get it

I also see how you treat her

I know you care about her, in a way you can't explain

I hope you would end up with her

But she had her heart broken before

Her heart ripped out from her chest

She has wounds and scars that fill her arms

Crying herself to sleep, every so often

But you're different, you care

Your soul is pure, you want to be with her

I can see that; I can understand you

But I also understand her point of view, she's my best friend

So, just don't hurt her, you'll be hurting me too

You had to leave

You ran out the door

You knew you couldn't stay

You knew I cared too much, so you left

Not turning back, you left without a sign

Leaving me to second-guess myself

Shattered to the ground

Your promises were hollow and empty

You grew cold, and scare

You knew I was better than you, so you always questioned me

Wondering why I was with you from the start

Why not someone else

So, you left, without a second glance

You shattered my heart, but you wanted me to shatter yours

My heart broke, you'd hoped it would have been yours

But life doesn't work that way

Not how we planned

You broke me free, cut my chains off

Rushing out that door, like you didn't know me at all

We don't text anymore, not like we used to

We both moved on with our lives

We're not as close anymore, you left before I did

We don't attend the same school, but we never planned to

I just didn't expect you to move so far

But that wasn't your fault

I think you knew that, I hope you're doing well now

I wonder if we will ever meet again

When you walked out that door, I thought I'd lose my mind

Left me shattered, with a heart so unkind

You didn't look back, you didn't think twice

Relief from the stress, but a painful sight

I didn't understand, why at that time

Your words, a betrayal, a heart that would leave

I saw you with her, a mirror image of me

But different, a replacement, a new spree

Your arms around her, a familiar embrace

I knew the truth, a painful, bitter taste

I watched you two walk, hand in hand

A love so made up, playing pretend

She cares for you, I can tell

But does she know you as I do?

Does she know your heart's goal?

You hurt others, carving for the love you never got

Scars on your heart, from the love that never came

So, you hurt others before you're the one to blame

You crave love, but never receive it

So, you play the game, with hearts that you deceive

A player, that's all you'll ever be

Leaving scars, and broken hearts, wild and free

When I was little, I wanted to be the same as everybody

When I was younger, I wanted to grow up

For adults to stop treating me like a child

When I was younger, I wanted to be like other kids

But I never wanted to play pretend

I was just like the boys, hanging with them

The girls were jealous of me, I got their attention

But never learned to be soft, always saying what's on my mine

When I grew up and got a little older

I learned from the girls, but I never dressed like them

I never wore makeup, never saw the point

I learned to be soft, maybe too soft

Getting hurt, giving myself away, not standing up for myself

I stopped saying the things on my mind

Sadness became my new normal, always stayed at home

Never going out

But I didn't want to be like the girls, I didn't want to be the same

All the girls were so mean, a bully to others

Girls got jealous, what a stupid thing

I didn't want to be like the boys, everyone was the same

For once, I wanted to be different

I wanted to be me, but I didn't know how

Who is that? How can I be myself?

I didn't know how to be me from the start

But I was always more like a tomboy from the start

I think I found inner peace, I feel like a child

I enjoy being with friends, and family as well

I need my alone time, to recharge my social battery

But I found my inner peace, I'm happy now

I'm chasing my goals, heading down the right path

I now understand my worth, value, and scars

My scars once meant the worst parts of me, now shine so bright

The scars are a reminder of my past life

I no longer overthink about the future

Only stepping forward, step by step

Day by day, I'm living in the present

A gift that I'll forever be grateful for

Save me from the darkness that consumes my soul

Show me pure love, and make me whole

I yearn to love with every beat of my soul

But fear of pain keeps me from chasing my heart's goal

I've built walls to shield my deepest scars

Afraid to love again, and face the same old wars

But I long for a love that's true and kind

The kind that lasts, a love that's one of a kind

I dream of a love that never fades

A love that grows stronger with each passing day

A bond that weathers every stormy hour

And in each other's arms, we find our peaceful sight

I want a love that understands and forgives

A love that holds me tight, and never lets me drift

Through every fight, we'll find our way back home

And in each other's love, our hearts will forever roam

I don't like being alone anymore, by myself at least

I want to be alone with friends, chatting to the very end

To play games, talk about life's hardest times

To be there for one another, despite the pain we face

A friendship that will never die, never fade, even in the nick of time

A best friend, but even more, a friendship that feels like family

Sharing our deepest thoughts and the fear we face

Through heartaches, and tragic times

I want friends that will always be by myself

Through heartbreaks, and painful scars

True friendship will never fade

A friendship that's pure and true, I hope for a friend through the bitter end

I wonder what it's like to be chosen

I wonder what it's like to be wanted

But I guess I will never change; I don't think I will

But I also wonder what it's like to be needed

To always know you can run to that same person

To know that person will never leave your side

I wonder what it's like to be needed

I wonder, I wonder, I wonder

I don't think I will ever get used to it

I don't think I will ever be me again

I don't think I'm brave enough

I know I'm not, but maybe I am

Maybe there's a part of me that will always be stronger, braver, free

A vision of me that doesn't care as much, that is not weak and sacred

And able to put herself out there

Maybe there's a part of me waiting to be free, waiting to be awaken

But I don't know how to

I don't understand how to spread my winds

How am I supposed to fly when I can't even walk?

How am I supposed to run when I can't even crawl?

I'm not the woman I want to be, not just yet

I want to be outgoing, and friendly, but I don't know where to start

Maybe I'm afraid to take the first step

Or I'm worried that people will judge

I'm not confident in myself, not just yet, but I hope I'll get there

Dear friend

I missed you; I thought I would never get over you

But I did, and I think you did too

I don't know when, but you did

I guess that's why you left

You didn't give me a head, you just walked out the door

I thought I had done something wrong; I didn't know what

But now I know I didn't and maybe you just needed some time alone

I hope you come back, and we can be friends again

I hear echoes in the darkness, the voices in my ear

I hear my heart beating quickly in my ear

My chest rose and fell slowly

I'm still, but the wind whispers secrets to me

I'm alone in this dark room, but I don't feel lonely

The moon is out, casting a soft glow

There's no one outside, but it feels so loud

I lay still in bed, staring at the wall, hoping to fall asleep

My mind is overflowing with thoughts, just like the ocean breeze

I hear the water, as I imagine the waves, crashing into each other

My parents chatting in the other room softly

My heart's beating softer, no longer in my ear

The sound of music from the living room, I soon fell asleep

It's 8 PM, I can't sleep

I can't move, I don't know why

Thoughts flood my mind, getting louder every time

It's 8:20 PM I still can't sleep

I'm staring at the ceiling now, not moving one bit

It's 8:30 PM, I still stay awake

So, I head to the living room, lay down on the couch

I start to close my eyes, laying there very still, not moving a muscle

It's 9 PM, I'm asleep, but my mind is still awake

I think I'm dreaming, but it feels so lively

Everybody's falling in love, but I'm falling apart

While others are in love, I'm struggling to be free

Love surrounds me everywhere I see, a constant reminder of the loneliness within me

A painful sight, a heart that's in vain

Everyone's falling head over heels in love, while I'm falling apart

Trust is a big thing, hard to earn, easy to lose

Yet I still trust, when people have broken it time after time

I still trust, wanting someone to keep their promises

I still trust despite the hurt and pain

Despite the broken promises, and the empty words

I still trust because I care, because I hope someone will keep
their word

I still trust because it's easier

But I can't do this anymore, I can't keep trusting

Every damn time, someone goes back on their words

It's like a sharp knife stabbing me, chipping a little part of me
away

Until there's nothing left

So, I can't trust, and maybe that's why I have trust issues

Or maybe deep down I don't want to get my hopes up

But too many people have broken their promises

And went back on their words

I can't trust, not for a while

Don't ask me to trust you

Because it's gone

My trust is gone

I think it was a few years ago

I remember staring into your promising eyes

We were star gazing, the moon shone so bring

You told me I was your moon, with delight

That you wanted me to stay

You told me you loved me, that you would always be near

But you had your fingers crossed

I remember your sweet smile when you held me tight

I remember the words you spoke into my ear

The way my heart beats only for you

The way you made me feel so safe

But that was your plan, wasn't it?

It was planned from the start, wasn't it?

You got me to trust, after I told me my back story

The reasons I don't trust and can't trust as easily

That was your plan, I didn't see your fingers crossed back then

You had me fooled

Just like when you told me you loved me

When you knew my heart beats only for you

You had your fingers crossed all along

I wonder what if we were just friends

Maybe things would be better

Maybe you wouldn't leave me heartbroken

Maybe I wouldn't want to hurt myself, even damn time

Maybe life would be better

You wouldn't know much about me, I wouldn't know much about you

We wouldn't get into fights, and you wouldn't break my heart

Maybe I wouldn't hate myself so damn much

Maybe we would still stay in touch

Maybe you would care more, you would get to know me better

Maybe I wouldn't cry myself to sleep

Maybe you would have paid more attention to me and cared more

What if we were just friends? What if I never knew you back then?

What if we left it at that? What if you never hurt me?

We stayed friends and left it at that

What if I never texted you back? What if we never chatted?

I would still be the same, the younger me with no depression

I knew the end was getting closer

But I thought we would grow older

But you, you will never have my heart

There's nothing new, whenever I'm alone

I don't look through our photographs, not anymore

I never like having photographs on my phone

But you convinced me to

But I deleted our photographs together, our memories too

It's funny because I don't even recognize myself anymore

I never hated you, I never hated things when I was with you

But I didn't know myself back then

I didn't know how much pain you would have caused

Painful scars and endless crying

I didn't know I was with someone who didn't mind hurting me

You acted differently with me versus your friends

You cared more about them, not as much as me

But I didn't hate you, I can't hate you anymore

You showed me the type of guys I shouldn't be with

The type of guys that only cares about their friends

And themselves, I didn't want to be ignored

But you ignored me anyway

He cared about having friends, about having the most friends

He cared about being liked, the most popular guy in school

But he ignored the people who cared, the person who cared the most

She gave too much of her time to the person that doesn't even care about her

These two people were in two different worlds

He wanted to be popular and cool

While she wanted to be seen and appreciated

Two different people that will never work

I don't know if I'm happy or sad

I don't know if I feel things anymore

I laugh when I want to cry, even when I'm sad

I don't know what that means

It will take a while before I trust in guys

Before I trust in anyone again

Because it seems like everyone I trusted in, has broken their promises

Going back on their words

So, the next guy or the next person

Please be patient with me

Please don't break your promise, and don't go back on your words

Because I had enough of people like that

I hope you had a great day; I hope everything's okay

Life wouldn't have been fun without you

I hope you know that I will always be here for you

Just call and I will pick up the phone

Just text and I will answer

Take your time to heal, relax your mind

You have time, I'll always be here waiting

Just give me a call, and I will be on my way

Tell them I was happy

Tell them my scars are now open

Tell them you didn't care, you didn't give a shit

That all of this was one huge lie

Tell them how I made you better

The way I made your life better

Because those are things you told me

Tell them how you watched me lose control of my mind

How I gave you everything, and you throw that away

Tell them how you stopped caring a while ago

The way you throw me out of your life like I was trash

Tell them how you watched me until I couldn't breathe

Tell me, how did you feel when you shattered my soul?

Did you enjoy the sound of my heart, as it lost control?

How did you relish the tears, that fell like the rain?

Did you bask in the pain, that you caused me to sustain?

You never told me the truth, just a web of lies

A dishonest game, where I was the prize

You never revealed, the secrets you shared

With family and friends, about the way you impaired

My trust, my love, my heart, you crushed them all

And yet, you acted like, you didn't hear my call

You pushed me aside, like a used, worn-out thing

While you prioritized others and made me feel like I nothing

Tell me, how did you feel, when you knew you'd broken me in two?

Did you feel a thrill, at the thought of my heart, shattered and blue?

You left me in pieces, like a puzzle on the floor

And walked away, like I was nothing more

Then a mere obstacle, a hindrance to your fun

A person who cared too damn much, my heart was torn apart

Like paper ripped out, torn to shreds

For loving you too deeply, for giving too much

But it's always the people who care more, that get punished in the end

I'm a mess, I overthink the little things in my head

But you seem to help me smooth my thoughts in my head, calming my nervous mind

I get so nervous whenever I look into your eyes

Lost in them, like time has stopped

I love the way you can't seem to find the right thing to say

I love the way; you can't keep your eyes off me

You're everything I want, but I didn't think I could have

You're everything I need to breathe, like my oxygen and my breath

I was lost in the haze of joy and delight

A dreamy world where love shone so bright

Cloud 9, where happiness was all around

But it was just a dreamy fantasy, a make-believe, an illusion of my mind

The person I thought you were, a figment of imagination

A creation of hope, a make-believe in my mind

I didn't see the darkness inside, the person you truly were at that time

You had no time for me, no love to shine

I lived in a world of make-believe

Where romance exists, but only in my dreams, I could breathe

But you remained unchanged, a constant heart of stone

Leaving me to face the lonely truth, alone

I'm glad you cried, even just a little

Because it means, that I was someone special to you, that you cared about

I'm happy you felt sadness, even just a little pain

It shows we were something, something that remained

I long to know that tears fell from your eyes

A sign that our love story still echoes in your mind

That you felt something when you were with me, a heartache
or a sting

Proof that our connection was more than just a fleeting thing

I want to know that you felt something, at least once, or more

A wave of sadness, a glimpse of what we had before

For in that pain, I find peace, a love that remains

A reminder that our love was more than just a lie, a love that
still sustains

I wonder if you think about me, I hope you do

I mean, I want you to, maybe once or twice, or even more

Because that would mean, we would have mutual feelings for each other

I wonder if you think about us sometimes

I wonder if the thought of my name crosses your mind

I wonder if you think about me like I think about you

I wonder if you ponder about us when we're apart, and together

I want you to think about me, to think about us

I want to be someone special to you, even if it's just for a while

So, do you think about me, like how I think of you?

Do you like me the way I want you to?

Oh I hope you do, I hope I'm someone special to you

She overthinks a lot, maybe too much at times

Her mind was like a battlefield, where criticism wore the crown

She struggles to stare at herself in the mirror, to smile with ease

Her reflection was a canvas, where flaws were expertly teased

"If only I were thinner," her mind whispers low

"If only my arms were smaller," the critiques start to grow

She was trapped in a cycle, of self-blame and shame

A never-ending game, for an unattainable frame

But even with time, she learned to stop

She learned to silence, the critic's relentless pace

Yet, the ghosts of old habits, still linger and sway

An eating disorder, a dangerous, unhealthy way

He wanted attention, she wanted someone who deeply cared

He wanted to make friends, to be the most popular, while she didn't care

He wanted to be well known, he wanted friends, too many of them

She just wanted someone to care, she wanted to be seen and heard

He wanted fame, and followers, she didn't care for those

He left her, heart shattered to the ground, while she cried

Not knowing why

He broke her heart, wanting to move on quickly

She took her time but understood why

Both of them were never meant to stay together, only to learn from one another

She gave herself away, too afraid to leave

He was too shallow, only caring for friends that didn't matter

Wanting to be known, while pushing what he had away

She didn't want those things, but it was a lesson learned

She knew she would find her love, someone who truly cares

Her one true love, she knew her heart would be found again

Her broken heart will mend

Two people meant to meet, but never meant to last

Only in each other's life to teach one another lessons

Maybe the two will meet again, but we'll never know

You knew the gift I wanted, without my knowledge

You got my attention, but it wasn't the present that won my heart's score

You were there for me, every time I needed a hand

A constant presence, that made me feel so grand

No one has ever cared for me like you did, with such kindness and grace

You showed me love, in every single place

I didn't need a gift, to know you truly cared

But you gave me one, to show me you're always there

Your thoughtfulness and love were so pure and true

It makes me feel special, and forever grateful to you

You're special to me, in ways I can't define

Forever in my heart, a love so divine

If you get the chance to love someone again

If you find yourself falling in love with someone

Fall in love with me, fall in love with my soul

I will love you in every way possible, let us fall in love with each other

We both know hurt, we both know pain

And even when we fight, we will always remain the same

So next time, if you find yourself falling in love with someone

Let it be with me, fall in love with me

My feelings for you, I dare not speak

Your friendship is a treasure, I don't want to throw it away

More than a friend, my heart beats for you

But fear of rejection, my words I hold true

You've been hurt before, and I don't know what to say

My emotions were silenced, in a secret way

I long for you to feel, the same love I do

But fear of heartache, my voice grows cold

In silence, I hope, someday you'll see

The love I have for you, and feel it too, wild and carefree

But until then, I'll lock my feelings away

And cherish our friendship, like a precious, burning flame

I like you, but I dare not tell

I like you, it's been a while

I know you inside and out, you can't play games with me

I know when you're not feeling yourself

And when you're feeling your best

Because I like you, like you, not just as a friend

I liked you for a long time now

But I dare not speak, for I don't know if you'll feel the same about me

Talk to me like you want to, like you need oxygen to breathe

Talk to me like I'm the only one you see

Talk about me to your friends and family, like I'm exactly what you need and want

Talk to me like you love me like you're head over heels in love with me

Talk to me like you want to, like you crave to

Talk to me like my name gives you butterflies

The thought of me, makes you smile so bright

Talk to me like you want to, like I'm on your mind morning and night

I like you, and that's not a lie

I liked you since childhood, but I dare not tell

I like you, you're my friend in crime

I like you, but I'm sure you know why

You're my friend, you'll never lie

I like you in many ways, I don't understand why

But I don't dare speak a word, I want to keep you as a friend

I dare not tell, in case our friendship ends

But I like you, like you, that's the bitter truth

But I'd been hurt many times, and I don't want our friendship
to end

Hoping someday, you'll feel the same

Until then, I'll stay by your side, in this secret pain

The sad truth is no one checks up on me

Unless I check up on them, text them first, or call

That's how I know I have no one

I don't know how to make friends, it never came naturally to me

I enjoy sitting by myself most of the time, but it's loneliness

The truth is, I feel lonely and sad inside, I feel like I'm trap

And can't fly free

Every time I try to make new friends

I'll always get scared and back down

It's also the fact that I don't want to be annoying or rude

I know I'm not, but it feels like I am

I mean, everyone has their friend group

And I'm stuck here, not knowing how to make any

I would like to be able to make friends without a care in the world

But mentally and physically I just can't

I like being with you, I like you in that scent

I don't understand why, I can't comprehend

I like you, in a way, I want to be your best friend

The one you go to, whenever you need a hand

I like you; I swear I do

I can't wrap my head around it, I can't comprehend

But I like you and that's the truth

In a way, I want to be your best friend

The one you go to, whenever you need a shoulder to cry on

I like you, you're my best friend

Near or far, you're always close, come what may

I like you, I don't quite understand

But I like you, like a best friend

I'm forgetting your face, I truly am

Thoughts of you, no longer consume my days

Your sorrow no longer brings me pain's dark ways

Your absence, once a hollowed ache

Now echoes silence, a heart that's awake

My joy, revived, like a blooming flower

My heart, mended, with each passing hour

My joy is restored, my heart is mended

Your name, once a trigger, a painful refrain

Now just a distant memory

I'm forgetting about you, the way you cause my heart pain

The way you cause me to be in shame

Someone who cares too damn much is always the problem

I learn that the hard way, a tough pill to swollen

Because I was the one who cared too damn much in every single place

I cared too damn much, and that's the truth

I cared too damn much, that's a hard pill to swollen

I learned my lesson, next time I'll not care that much

Or maybe it would be better if I stop caring

Because I cared too damn much, and now I'm lost in my way

"You were the right person at the wrong time"

At least that's what you told me

"I was the right person at the wrong time"

I kept repeating those words in my head

You wanted me to hold on, to believe in our fate

But I see now, it was just a way to delay the weight

But you're not the "right person at the wrong time"

I didn't know why I didn't see it sooner

I needed time, I needed to heal and mend

To heal from the pain you cause, to renew and learn

I needed space, and now I know why

"Right person, wrong time", A phrase used too many damn time

If you were truly the one, you would have stayed

Through every storm, through every shade

But you left, and now I see

That "right person, wrong time" is just an excuse, a fantasy

But I wonder if I was the "right person at the wrong time" for you

Do you miss me?

Did you love me with all your heart and soul?

I hope you wanted me, to be in your life

Do you still miss me, was I enough for you?

Here's the truth, she tried her best

And every single time she has fallen, she has gotten back up

But sometimes life is too much, and the truth is, most time she was not brave enough

Most time, she's just a girl, trying her best to live in the hopes of a better day

Her parents didn't understand her at times

She never needed them to understand her, she didn't blame them

She has friends, but maybe that's the problem

Her friends taught her, how to be soft, maybe too soft

Life has been feeling tough for her lately

She can't look at herself in the mirror, without a genuine smile

Her mind is filled with doubts, and she overthinks a lot

She's starting to think, that her best will never be enough for people

For her parents

I know people come and go

It's been planted in my head since I was younger

It's been rooted in my mind

I know people come and go

There are seasons for people to stay

But can you be the one to stay?

Can I just hold onto you for a little while longer?

Can we be there for each other?

Stone Cold is a name that fits so well

A heart that's hardened, a soul that's compelled

To apologize, to utter empty words

But hollow promises, that leave me unheard

Your regrets, an echo that resonates deep

A meaningless murmur, that my heart can't keep

When you speak, it's just an unoccupied sound

A promise unfulfilled, an unbound love

But when I apologize, my heart is true

I meet you with sincerity and a love that shines through

No empty echoes, no hollow refrain

Just a genuine heart, that beats with love and pain

I'm on cloud nine whenever I look at you

I'm daydreaming, you're so perfect, you're so kind

I'm speechless whenever I look at you

Your eyes shine under the bright sun like diamonds sparkling in the dark

Your hair moves like waves under the cool breeze

You smile at me, and I don't know what to do

I utter the words "How could someone look this handsome?"

You didn't hear me; my heart was pounding when you came closer

You kissed me on my hand, then you kissed me on the lips

I remember staring at you like I'm the luckiest person in the world

It's the quietest time when I feel the loudest

My deep thoughts in my head screaming at me, scratching my skull

Sometimes I feel like I can't breathe, the words are too damn loud

I feel like I'm drowning in a sea of thoughts, where I'm trying to swim

And grasp for air, but something is pulling me down

Underneath the salty water, it feels so cold

My lungs are burning in the flames, I'm slowly losing control

My energy slowly deteriorates, I wave my hands in the air

Shouting and screaming, yelling for help

But my mouth is duck-taped shut

And there's no one around to save me

It's the quietest time when I feel the loudest

My deep thoughts in my head screaming at me, scratching my skull

Sometimes I feel like I can't breathe, the words are too damn loud

Let me hate you, yet I still adore

Why can't I despise you, like I've been ignored?

I claim to be indifferent, but deep down I confess

I yearn for your attention, your tender caress

I long for you to notice my absence, my pain

As I felt yours, like an ache that refuses to disappear

Why can't I hate you, after all the tears I've cried?

After all the time we shared, I still can't deny it

My heart remains the same, though broken and worn

No longer beating for you, and no longer believing in love

I wished you'd seen me as I saw you

Notice my heart, once full, now broken in two

You're like a golden ray, shining bright and bold

Illuminating my world, young and old

Whenever I gaze at you, my heart takes flight

You light up the darkness, like stars shining so bright

With just one glance, my mood begins to shift

Your smile, a ray of sunshine, banishes the rift

You're my guiding light

My golden ray, that makes everything all right

I'm forgettable, or so I've come to believe

A fleeting thought, easily dismissed, it seems

My friends only reach out when I initiate the conversation

No one notices when I'm struggling with my emotions, devotion

I've learned to wear a mask, a disguise so well

To appear strong, even when I'm falling apart within

To smile, when tears are streaming down

A master of deception, where my true self, is unseen, and unheard

Perhaps that's why I'm always the one to make the first move

Why no one thinks to check in, to see how I'm doing

I've become a ghost, invisible and grey

Forgettable, just like I've always feared, every day

If a relationship means being ignored

Being left all alone

Standing in the cold by myself

If a relationship means not caring at all, not giving a damn

Not trying your best

If it means freezing in the cold while you're inside

In the warm house

If a relationship means not caring

Crying myself to sleep every day

If a relationship means paying more attention to your phone

Paying more attention to your friends

Leaving me alone and wondering if I'm truly happy

Because you see me smiling doesn't mean I'm warm

If a relationship means getting heartbroken repeatedly

Feeling isolated and disconnected

From the world

I don't think I want to be in a relationship

Blame me for your sadness

Blame me for your pain

Blame me because you needed to feel better about yourself

Blame me because you needed to feel like the victim

Blame me for not being in your life

Blame me, blame me, blame me all you want

But don't blame me for not being there

Staying by your side when you needed it most

Don't try to convince your friends and family

That I wasn't there, because I was

You can blame me all you want, push me aside

But you won't know my side of the story

The painful truth

You won't know how I had to create two versions of myself

You won't know the true me

So, blame me all you want

Blame me for how I made you feel

Blame me for your sadness

Blame me for your stress

But don't blame me for your misunderstanding

It's the damn phones

It seems fine, but I see how people act

With friends or not

It's the damn phones, it has always been the case

We're not able to go into a conversation without our phones

We're always on them, it's the damn phones

Rotting our brain, we no longer have human connection or human touch

It's the damn phone, it has always been the damn phones

You will never know me, not truly

I showed you glimpses, but only briefly

When I'm with others, I keep my distance

But with you, I was a fool, I got too close to the flames

I got too close to the flames, and I got burned instead

But was that me? Was that me who got burned and lost it all?

I made two versions of myself, to keep me safe, and you happy

But you were never truly gonna be happy

I was with you but didn't see the truth in you

I mean I saw it, but didn't run, I stayed, helping you aim the gun at me

A gun to my head, a slow and painful demise

A tragic story, where I compromised

I was never gonna be truly yours

And you were never gonna be truly mine

I was never gonna be your queen

You were never gonna be my king

I was never gonna be your princess

And you were never gonna be my prince

But we had that for a short time

It felt so long

But I'm grateful that you ended things

I'm truly grateful, you needed to get a grasp on your life

And I needed to focus on mine

You had to learn to treat people right

And I needed to learn to say the things on my mind

So, we were never meant for each other

We were never meant to stay

Only to learn from the pain and hurt, to grow, but not together, in vain

He told me, he loved me more times than I could count

That he would always be there

Through the ups and down

I was a fool for believing all those lies

I was a fool to believe, to trust in empty promises

For I didn't feel loved, only unheard and neglected

He never showed affection, unless I begged for scraps

No time, no attention, unless I chased the cracks

The memory of loneliness still haunts me

A ghost that lingers, a heart that still aches

But the pain subsides, now that we're apart

For I know I deserved more, a love that's in my heart

I recall the tears, the sorrow, and the pain

But also, the strength, that emerged like summer rain

For I knew I'd be fine, that I'd rise above

For words without action is nothing at all

I can no longer meet my gaze with a smile

Not like I once did, with an unbridled style

The reflection stares back, a stranger to me

A familiar face, yet I don't know who she is

I've lost the carefree grin, the effortless delight

Now, my eyes betray, a hollow haunted light

I feel disconnected, a soul standing in the cold

Isolated from the world, with nowhere to go

But paradoxically, solitude brings me peace

In the darkness, I find solace, my spirit releases

The chill of loneliness, that once made me shiver

Now, it's a sensation that makes me feel alive and carefree

In the silence, I find myself again

A place where I feel whole, and renewed

I'm starting to think, I don't need the crowd

From in solitude, I find my true self, my identity, unbound

It was all a deception, a made-up lie

I wanted to believe you, I still do

To give you the benefit of the doubt

But then, I'll be lying to myself

I don't want to call you a liar, but you are

Was anything you said true?

Did you feel the way I did?

I wanted to give you the benefit of the doubt so many times

And I did, more times than I could count

So, I'll just have to call you a liar

While you walk out that door

Leaving me in pieces, slowly tearing myself apart

It was a lie

A made-up tale

Something I tell myself without fail

To have hope, under the stars

Hoping for the best without any scars

But little did I know, it was a trap

Scars that are left deeply carved into my bones

Bloody cuts that will forever be left unhealed

You never knew the hobbies I had

You never asked how my day went

You never knew the pain, the scars, the tears I cried

Yet you knew me, but not the true me

You never tried to understand me, to comprehend my thoughts

The way I did with you, the way I was with you

You couldn't wrap your head around it

So you left instead, without a doubt, without fail

You never cared to know me

Not wanting my phone number

You wanted me to text you

Yet, you hated when people called

I cared about you, with every inch of me

While you didn't care at all

But I guess that's how people are

Only caring if it benefits them

I want to tell you everything, the ups and downs

I want to tell you how I feel, inside and out

I want to come running home to you, after work

Despite my doubts, I want to tell you about my day

I want you, but I can't find the right words to say

I want you, more than I need you

I desire to have you, more times than I can count

I need you, you're my oxygen

Without you, I can't breathe properly

I'm surrounded by romance, everywhere I go

I watch people holding hands on the streets, at the beach

Romance surrounds me, no matter my mood

When I drift to sleep

I dream of having someone special

Yet, life sets in

I don't want that, the perfect romance on screens

I hate depending on someone else

And slowly I'm starting to think romance doesn't truly exist

Not at all

I want to know you, inside and out

I want to be the person you come running home to without a doubt

The one that's there for you no matter what

I want you to want me despite our broken hearts

I want us to fall in love, no matter the cost

To be there for each other, despite our flaws

To hold one other through life's hardship

Just two broken hearts, trying to love once more

I want you to want me

I want you to need me but for the right reasons

I want you to call

To text me, but not because I asked

I want you to check up on me

To ask me, how my day went

I want you to want me

But I don't need you to need me

As I approach 22, I'm left feeling unfulfilled

Schools taught me algebra and essay-writing skills

Reading endless papers, not knowing how to comprehend them

And neglected life's essential lessons

Teachers urged me to "have fun"

Yet my days were filled with solving for X and endless math problems

No financial classes, no practical life advice

How can I "have fun" when my days are consumed

By exhausting school schedules and parental expectations?

From 4 AM to 6 PM, I'm trapped in a never-ending cycle

Grades, pleasing parents, the pressure keeps getting heavier

Now, as I reach adulthood, I feel lost and uncertain

What have I achieved; do I still have time?

The void within me grows, a nagging sense of stagnation

Schools taught me to stay in my lane

To complete all my homework before the deadlines

To pressure myself into being the best

Always wanting to achieve better grades

To please my parents and my teachers too

Yet my friends urged me to have fun

To not have my head in the books all the damn time

But how can that be possible?

How can I have a work-life balance in that sense?

From heading to school at 8 AM

Coming back home at 4 PM

And now that I have a part-time job

There will be no time to spare

It's the endless cycle, of getting work done

No time for free time, to rest

Just work, work, work, all day, every day

Two people living inside my head

Two different parts of me, screaming to get out

One's fighting to come out

While the other is holding the door shut tight

One feel numb to the touch

While the other feels everything to the touch

One that cares a little too much

And the other, not at all, or a little less

But both hate me

The reflation I see in the mirror

She hates me

She wonders if anyone hates her too

Maybe her friends

Or her parents too

But one thing's for sure

She hates her reflation in the mirror

You told me to reflect on myself

So, I did just that

I can say all the thoughts in my mind

But you wouldn't mind that

You told me to reflect on my life

So, I did just that

I will say the things in my head

But you wouldn't be afraid

I feel lost in this world I call my home

Nowhere to go, no one to call my own

I feel like my goals and dreams are crushed

The voices inside my head, so loud, so rush

I tried pushing them away but failed, time after time

I'm tired of the mess I made

Not able to do anything right

You tried to shape me into the perfect human

But I'm not perfect at all

I don't have a perfect body

Not a perfect soul

I don't have a perfect heart

Mine was broken from the start

Two people living inside my head

Two different parts of me, screaming to get out

One's fighting to come out

While the other is holding the door shut tight

One feels numb to the touch

While the other feels everything to the touch

One that cares a little too much

And the other, not at all, or a little less

But both hate me

The reflation I see in the mirror

She hates me

She wonders if anyone hates her too

Maybe her friends

Or her parents too

But one thing's for sure

She hates her reflation in the mirror

Maybe one day, when everything's right

Maybe one day, when the stars align

Maybe one day, when the moon calls out my name

Maybe one day, when I can look at myself

In the mirror, and smile

Maybe one day, we will meet

You will get to know me

And I will get to know you

You'll ask for my number, and I will blush

Maybe one day, you will take me by the hand

Smile, and lead me to dance

Maybe one day, I will find a man that's just right

I want to call my other side out

To take on the pain, because I don't want to

To hold my hand, knowing there's someone there

I want to love, love with everything I have

I want to be loved, loved by the right man

I want to know myself inside and out

But for right now

I want to call my other side, out

I watch as the world goes by

People hand in hand, smiling at the sand

I want that, the thing that makes me different from the rest

I want the thing I don't have

For the void of loneliness to fade

I want to know that I'll be okay in the end

I want to be loved and have a love that will hold me tight

I want the right guy to treat me just right

She stays in her room

Not wanting to get out of her house

She wants to head out with friends

But none of them wants her around

Her mind filled with deep thoughts

The voices in her head, getting louder

Every single day, every second

Telling them to "shut up" is no use

But she tells them to "shut up" anyways

Knowing that no matter what

The voices will still stay

Getting louder every damn time

Hoping one day, it will just stop

Hoping one day, the pain will just grow cold

That someone will help make it stop

And the pain will fade away

She loved a boy

She loves with all her heart

But her heart got torn apart in the end

So, she built a tall wall

Hoping someday someone will break it

Hoping one day, she would be able to love again

To love herself again

And someone would treat her right, scars and all

Broken hearts are my artful obsession

A mirrored echo of my inner tension

Maybe it's because I've felt shattered inside

My heart ripped apart from the start

I feel lost and alone

Like I'm trying to survive in the deep seas

I see an island far, and paddling to it

But never reaching

As I swim closer, it moves farther

I'm cold, trying to stay calm

But chills of darkness hold me tight

Not letting go of me, not wanting to lose sight

I feel myself shake, as I lose control

Life is a damn ocean

A deep, cold ocean with nowhere to go

I feel lost, and cold

Loneliness covers me in a blanket

I'm numb to the touch

I don't know who I am

I can't stare at myself in the mirror

I don't feel pretty but not ugly

I feel like a mess, a fuck up mess

I don't know where to go, the place I call home

I'm not there or here, just floating through life

I want a healthy body

A happy soul

I want my heart to heal and mend

But mine was broken from the start

I can't sleep in the dark

My fears come out to play

The deep thoughts drowning the sound around me, out

It's dark out, everyone's asleep

But I stay awake, wanting to sleep too

But fearing the worst in my head

I talk to the monsters under my bed

Knowing the monsters are my friends

I talk to them, telling them my problems and fear

I talk about my day, the life I have

I feel a chill down my spine

And stop, knowing I'm no longer myself

I wish you knew me better

I wish you wanted to get to know me

I wish you wanted to text me, to check up on me, to call

I wish you wanted to spend time with me

I wish you cared about me a little more

I wish you didn't play with my heart

Because my heart was already broken

And torn apart

I tell myself to be kind

To always be filled with joy

I tell myself to always stay happy

That I should brighten people's day

I tell myself to stay calm

Not to stress over spilled milk

That I should be happy inside and out

To fit into crowds, and make friends

I tell myself that I will always be me

The same me, that was born into this world

But that was a lie, I feel myself changing

Day by day, I'm a different version of myself now

We're in school for 8 hours

Solving for X, for countless hours

Dealing with math problems

When we can't even deal with ours

2 hours of homework turns into 4 hours

"Have fun" teachers say

"Don't take life so seriously" others say

But all we do is work, nothing else

I overthink the little things in my head

Because that's what I do best

Despite the pain I'd been through

My fear seems to always hold me back

And my deep thoughts comes to play

I can't sleep an hour of the day

The voices getting louder day by day

Screaming in my face

I can't stop it now, no matter what I do

Telling them to shut up won't help now

But I do it, anyway, knowing the words won't go to waste

Hoping it will work out, someday

The words in my head, getting louder day by day, burning brighter

Surrounding me like wildfire

The flames roaring louder, burning hotter

And brighter every damn time

I feel cold now, lost in the flames

A chill runs down my spine

Always wasting my damn time

Not giving me a dime

Holding me tight, until I can't breathe

The voices are getting louder, I wanna cry

Someone, please hold me tighter

Until the pain subsides

You built me up, only to destroy me in the end

Gave me hope, then took control

You nurtured my trust, just to rip it away

Leaving me shattered, torn apart, with nothing to say

You played the innocent role, while I bore the pain

Your careless actions are forever in vain, scars deep in my bones

You played the victim, but I see the truth

You're the coward, responsible for my youth

Screaming in my head

Dreaming in my bed

Pulling me in like an invisible tread

With words left unsaid

Thoughts in my head

You left me on read

Feeling the monsters under my bed

Crying and whipping instead

The monsters came out to play

Staring up at the sky

Forgetting all my fears

The stars shine bright and pure

Their light soft and enchanting cure

I'm cured and secured now

Words left unsaid

Free from the fears in my head

Standing there, with my bright brown hair

Staring at the bright blue sky

Wondering if I will ever be enough

Life seems so difficult and I feel cold inside

All alone in this way, just trying to find my way back home

I can't seem to find my way back

The thoughts are getting louder day by day

All the things I want to say, seem to always go to waste

The thoughts are far away, unreachable

Always holding me one step back

I can't find the right words to say

That I'm trying, but crying deeply inside

I was just a game to you

You made me feel ashamed in that kind of way

I can only blame myself in the end

What a fool I've been

You left me, unseen, only part of your routine

I was only seventeen, you left me heartbroken

Rushed out the door, not a phone call away anymore

Left standing there in between worlds

A fool I've been, an emotionally stupid little me

I don't want to miss you, anymore

I miss you a little less day by day

My broken heart healed; my shattered soul mended

Revealing myself anew

Healing from the blue

I missed myself more than I did you

My soul roaring louder than ever before

Hold me tight

Until you can feel my breath on your pale skin

Hug me close, close enough to tell me you want me

That I was the best thing in your life

Love me, love me in ways you never thought possible

With every scar, every fear, every fibre

Just all of you

Look me in the eyes, like you did the first time we met

Stay with me a little while longer

Tell me stories, and jokes, make me smile like you back then

Hold me tight for the very last time

I'll always be by your side

Milton Keynes UK
Ingram Content Group UK Ltd.
UKHW020406021124
450424UK00014B/1459